CELEBRATE
HOLIDAYS

Celebrate Tet

Laura S. Jeffrey

A dancer wearing a mask celebrates Tet.

Enslow Publishers, Inc.
40 Industrial Road
Box 398
Berkeley Heights, NJ 07922
USA

http://www.enslow.com

Library of Congress Cataloging-in-Publication Data

Jeffrey, Laura S.
   Celebrate Tet / Laura S. Jeffrey.
    p. cm. — (Celebrate holidays)
   Includes bibliographical references and index.
   ISBN-13: 978-0-7660-2775-6
   ISBN-10: 0-7660-2775-9
     1. Vietnamese New Year—Juvenile literature. 2. Vietnamese New Year—United States—Juvenile literature. I. Title.
   GT4905.J44 2007
   394.261—dc22

                          2006031922

Printed in the United States of America

10 9 8 7 6 5 4 3 2 1

Illustration Credits: AA World Travel Library/Alamy, p. 50; Associated Press, pp. 28, 31, 34, 35, 36, 42, 69, 76, 83, 84; John Berry/Syracuse Newspapers/ The Image Works, p. 45; Private Collection/The Bridgeman Art Library Nationality, p. 52; Gerard Burkhart/AFP/Getty Images, p. 66; Corel Corporation, p. 85; Bob Daemmrich/The Image Works, p. 71; © Dbimages/Alamy, p. 57; Enslow Publishers, Inc., p. 18; Mary Evans Picture Library/The Image Works, p. 16; Tran Dinh Hiep/Vietnamese Wikipedia, p. 26; iStockphoto.com/Anthony Brown, p. 78; iStockphoto.com/Peter Fuchs, p. 86; iStockphoto.com/Matthew Ragen, p. 33; © 2007 Jupiterimages, p. 88; Truong Minh-Duc, p. 48; Hoang Dinh Nam/AFP/Getty Images, p. 61; Tho Nau/Vietnamese Wikipedia, p. 27; Michael Newman/Photo Edit, p. 20; Nicholas Pitt, p. 1; Shutterstock, pp. 4, 5, 9, 10, 12, 21, 37, 53, 64, 65, 79, 80.

Cover Illustration: Nicholas Pitt.

CONTENTS

A rice field in Asia

Ancient Tradition

Long, long ago, the devil ruled the earth. The people worked hard all year farming the land, but they did not have enough to eat because the devil took all the rice and other crops for himself. Buddha came down from heaven to help the people. He told them how to fool the devil so that they could keep the crops for themselves. The tricks worked, and the devil became angry. He took all the land so that the people could no longer plant anything.

Buddha again came down from heaven. He told the people to gather gold and offer it to the devil in exchange for a small plot of land. They would use the land to plant bamboo trees. The trees would belong to the devil, but the land under the trees' shadows would belong to the people.

The devil agreed to the deal, and the bamboo trees were planted. They grew so tall and abundant that eventually all the land in the village fell under their shadows. The people now could plant plenty of rice and other crops to eat.

The devil was very angry that he had been tricked yet again. He and his army invaded the village, but Buddha showed the people how to protect themselves and the trees. The devil and his followers were defeated, and the devil was banished to the sea. However, he was allowed to return to the village every year to visit his ancestors' graves.[1]

The Beginning of Tet

This legend has been handed down in Vietnam from generation to generation. It tells the story of how Tet began. But when did the Vietnamese people first start celebrating the holiday? No one really knows for sure.

Who was Buddha?

Buddha is not a name but a title. It means "one who is awake."[2] Buddha was born as Siddhartha Gautama in Nepal more than twenty-five hundred years ago. His family was royalty, but Buddha became aware of the pain and suffering in the world. This caused him to wonder about the meaning of life. Eventually, he left home and began to seek the truth. One day, he sat underneath a tree and vowed he would not leave until he had become enlightened. This meant that he would understand life as deeply as possible. After forty days under the tree, Buddha reached enlightenment.

Buddha traveled throughout India seeking to spread understanding. Buddha did not claim any special powers. He was simply a human being who had become enlightened.

Those who practice Buddhism seek to be free from greed, hatred, and ignorance, and filled with wisdom and compassion.

Vietnam is an ancient country where many people believe in myths and legends. According to Vietnam legend, the country was founded when Lac Dragon Lord, the dragon king, emerged from the sea. He married Au Co, who has been described as a fairy or birdlike creature. The couple had many sons who became kings, ruling over the land for thousands of years. Meanwhile, Lac Dragon Lord returned to the sea. This myth is very important to the Vietnamese because it is the story of creation.

The Reverend Dominic Nguyen is pastor of Sacred Heart Catholic Church in Dayton, Ohio. He said Tet has its roots in ancient Buddhism, but it is an important holiday for all Vietnamese, primarily those who are of the Catholic faith in America.[3]

"Carvings . . . dating from 500 to 1000 B.C. suggest that Tet was celebrated at least that far back," said Ellen L. Kronowitz, a professor of education at California State University who visited Vietnam. "The exact origin, however, is unknown. One can speculate that the renewal marked by the arrival of spring was a cause for the celebration."[4]

Spring is particularly special to Vietnam because of its long history of farming. The majority

After thousands of years, most of Vietnam continues to be farmland.

of the country is rural, and for thousands of years the people have farmed the land to survive. The most commonly grown crops are rice, corn, black beans, and sweet potatoes.[5] Tet usually coincides with a break in the farming schedule, so it is an opportunity for everyone to relax and celebrate.

Many people work in rice paddies, wetlands where rice is grown.

Vietnam

Vietnam has been known by many different names during its long history, including Van Lang, Nam Viet, and French Indochina. In fact, it has been called "Vietnam" consistently only since the end of World War II. It is long and narrow in shape, but thicker at its curved top and bottom, and is often described as looking like a stretched-out "S."

Vietnam shares borders with China, Laos, and Cambodia. The coastline stretches from the Gulf of Tonkin down to the South China Sea and the Gulf of Thailand. The country features rugged terrain with dense forests and many mountains.

Typically, the weather is subtropical or temperate. The country also experiences two monsoon seasons: the winter monsoon, from October to April, and the southwestern monsoon, from May to September.[6]

Like many Asian countries, the Vietnamese do not use the solar calendar, also known as the Gregorian calendar, to determine days. The Gregorian calendar divides time into 365 days for a year, with every fourth year, on even years, being a leap year of 366 days. Instead, the Vietnamese use the lunar calendar. In the Vietnamese lunar calendar, year one corresponds to 2637 B.C.

Vietnam is a mountainous land with rolling hills
like these located in the town of Sa Pa.

Lunar Calendar

The lunar calendar follows the stages, or phases, of the moon. The Vietnamese use these phases to determine when each new month begins. The earth orbits, or moves around, the sun. The moon orbits the earth. As the moon orbits the earth from west to east, it is illuminated in varying degrees by the sun. This is a continuous process, but the process is broken down into eight phases.

The first phase is the new moon. This is when the moon is not visible in the sky at all. This is because the side of the moon that is not illuminated by the sun is facing the earth. The second phase is waxing crescent. This is when a sliver of the right side of the moon can be seen. Waxing means increasing. So in the next few phases, even more of the moon can be seen in the sky.

The third phase is called the first quarter moon. In this phase, the right half of the moon can be seen. The fourth phase is the waxing gibbous moon. Now, more than half of the moon can be seen. By the fifth phase, or full moon, the entire moon can be seen in the sky.

As the moon continues its orbit, the illumination begins to decrease, or wane. The sixth phase is called the waning gibbous. Much, but not all, of the moon can be seen in the sky. The seventh phase is the last quarter moon. Now, only the left half of the moon can be seen.

Next comes the waning crescent. In this eighth and final phase, only a sliver of the left side of the moon can be seen. After the waning crescent, the lunar cycle begins again with the new moon, when the moon is not visible at all.

It takes anywhere from twenty-seven to twenty-nine days for one lunar cycle. This means a lunar month typically is shorter than a month on the Gregorian calendar. Each lunar month begins with the sighting of the waxing crescent moon after the new moon. Every third year, the Vietnamese add an extra month between its third and fourth months to keep the lunar year more in sync with the Gregorian calendar.[7] Tet usually falls sometime between January 19 and February 20.

Months, Years, and the Zodiac

Vietnamese do not divide time into centuries. Instead, they use units of sixty years called *hoi*. Each hoi consists of six ten-year cycles, called *can*, and five twelve-year cycles, called *ky*. Because of this system, the same combination of names is never produced twice. Each year is known by both its can and ky names.

The can names are as follows: water in nature (*giap*), water in the home (*at*), lighted fire (*bih*), latent fire (*dinh*), wood (*mau*), wood prepared to burn (*ky*), metal (*canh*), wrought metal (*tan*), virgin land (*nham*), and cultivated land (*quy*).[8]

The ky names are for animals in the Buddhist zodiac. The Vietnamese believe that long, long ago, the Jade Emperor, or ruler of heaven, organized a race for all of the animals in nature. He then created a calendar based on the first twelve winners, in the order in which they finished. The order is as follows: rat (*ty*), water buffalo (*suu*), tiger (*dan*) cat (*mao*), dragon (*thin*), snake (*ty*), horse (*ngo*), goat (*mui*), monkey (*than*), rooster (*dau*), dog (*tuat*), and pig (*hoi*).[9]

People are said to possess similar traits to the animal that corresponds to the year they were born. For example, Vietnamese born in the Year of the Rooster are believed to be outgoing and interesting, excellent organizers, sociable, perceptive, and loyal.[10] Those born during the Year of the Monkey are considered gamblers and risk-takers.[11] People born in the Year of the Horse are said to enjoy being in the spotlight and are hardworking and honest.[12] Know anyone born in 2006, the Year of the Dog? They likely will be loyal and friendly.[13]

玉
皇

The Jade Emperor governs the heavens and created the Buddhist zodiac.

The Vietnamese people do not celebrate birthdays on the day they actually were born. Instead, everyone turns one year older on Tet. So the holiday is not merely a new year celebration. It is also one big birthday party. In fact, Tet is so much more than that. The holiday, which also pays tribute to ancestors and is an opportunity to show family members love and affection, is at the very core of the Vietnam culture.

Antoinette Nguyen and her husband, Cong Nguyen, met in 1982 in Virginia after leaving Vietnam. They were married the following year. They are now both happy and proud United States citizens. Yet they never want to forget their country of origin.

In particular, they do not want to forget Tet. Tet is the most important holiday in the Nguyens' homeland. It is a spiritual as well as a cultural and national holiday. The Vietnamese pay respect to heaven, and there are official ceremonies to thank heaven as well as the national founders.

The Nguyens have passed down the traditions of the holiday to their three children, who were all born in the United States.

"I never intended to forget or deny my heritage," Antoinette Nguyen said. "Tet is sacred. It defines our identity."[14]

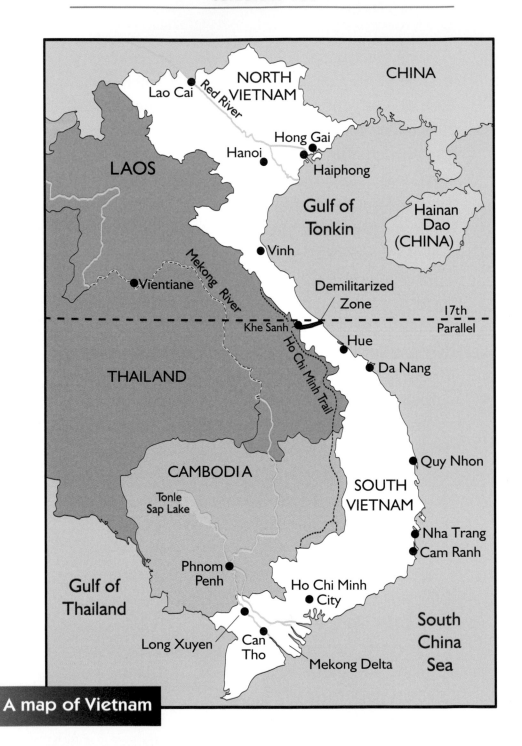

CHINA

NORTH VIETNAM

Lao Cai

Red River

LAOS

Hong Gai

Hanoi

Haiphong

Gulf of Tonkin

Hainan Dao (CHINA)

Vinh

Mekong River

Vientiane

Demilitarized Zone

17th Parallel

Khe Sanh

Hue

THAILAND

Ho Chi Minh Trail

Da Nang

CAMBODIA

Tonle Sap Lake

Quy Nhon

SOUTH VIETNAM

Nha Trang

Cam Ranh

Phnom Penh

Ho Chi Minh City

Gulf of Thailand

Long Xuyen

Can Tho

Mekong Delta

South China Sea

A map of Vietnam

Tet celebrates ancestors, family, and friendship. The holiday is filled with hope for good luck and prosperity in the year that lies ahead. The full name of the holiday, Tet Nguyen Dan, means "the first morning of the first day of the new period."[15]

Unlike New Year's Day in the United States, Tet does not fall on the same day each year. But the traditions and legends have been passed down for generations. The special holiday is believed to be as old as the country itself.

This family prays before an altar to their ancestors.

Honoring the Living and the Dead

Pretend for a moment that every member of your family celebrates his or her birthday on the same day. Now think about the way your family usually marks Mother's Day, Father's Day, Christmas or Hanukkah, Easter or Passover, and New Year's Day. Add all the parties together and what do you get? Tet. The holiday officially lasts for three days, but many Vietnamese celebrate for the entire week. Tet is a time for family, goodwill, and renewal, and it has great significance in the Vietnamese culture. It is a special and sacred holiday.

"Tet is a time we gather as a nuclear family to honor our living parents and deceased ancestors," said Antoinette Nguyen, who arrived in the United States in 1975 as a refugee of the Vietnam War. She and her husband, who is also Vietnamese, have raised their children to know about the ancestral homeland. "My children ought to know and maintain our roots, our tradition, and our culture," Nguyen said.[1]

Nguyen grew up in Vietnam with an older brother in a strict but loving family just outside of Saigon. "My mother valued education highly, so she sacrificed tremendously to send us to the best school in town," Nguyen recalled. "Our formal education was in French. Our generation was mostly bilingual, for that matter. You can say we inherited a good balance between these two cultures."[2]

Nguyen said that when she was a child, "I always looked forward to Tet. The ambiance— it was so festive outside and inside the home."[3]

On their Tet celebrations, Nguyen and her family attended Catholic Mass first thing in the morning. Then they visited with her mother's parents, or her maternal grandparents, who lived next door. "We went over with our parents to wish them happy new year," she said. "The tradition demanded that the wishes be presented by order of generation, meaning my parents presented their wishes to grandpa and grandma before we did ours."[4]

Nguyen and her family then traveled to the country to visit with her father's parents, or her paternal grandparents. "We spent the whole day . . . eating special foods and enjoying the day without being scolded because, out of superstition, the adults tried to avoid unhappy moments on Tet for fear they would occur more often during the new year," she said.[5]

Nguyen has special memories of playing all day, either cards or a board game in which she and the other children bet small amounts of money. "This was my favorite game," she said. "It was so much fun, and the only time of the year we were allowed to gamble."[6]

Chau Huu Tran is an engineer for the United States Department of Justice in Washington, D.C. He, too, is a refugee of the Vietnam War. Tran grew up in Saigon with his two sisters and parents.

"I grew up in the city so every Tet, I loved to go to the countryside to visit my grandparents," he recalled. "I enjoyed the country view and the environment—cool weather and fishing—but

What's in a Name?

In the United States and other Western countries, people are known by their given name first and then their family name, or surname. But Vietnamese names usually start with the surname, followed by an optional middle name and then the given name. This is because in the Southeast Asian country, more emphasis is placed on the family than on individuality.[7]

There are only a few hundred different surnames in Vietnam, so many people have the same surname but are not related. The most common Vietnamese surname is Nguyen. Tran is another common surname.[8]

Most children have the same surname as their father. Sometimes people combine the father's and mother's surnames, and the children have a double surname.

The Vietnamese do not name their children after relatives or friends; this is considered disrespectful. Instead, names are chosen because they sound beautiful. A girl might be named Cuc, for chrysanthemum, or Hoa, for flower. Popular names for boys are Hung, which means hero, and Tuan, which means handsome. Popular names for either boys or girls include Ha, for river, and Hai, for ocean.

On the other hand, some Vietnamese purposely pick ugly-sounding names for their children. They fear that if they give a child a beautiful name, he or she will become ill or will be kidnapped by devils.[9]

the most important thing was to [be around my] grandparents."[10]

Just as people who celebrate other holidays prepare in advance for them, the Vietnamese spend days getting ready for the Tet celebration. However, they usually do not begin preparations until the week before. A popular legend is that Three Kitchen Gods, or *Tao Quan*, observe everything that happens in the kitchen. On the twenty-third day of the final month of the lunar year, the kitchen gods depart for heaven to report on the year's activities to the Jade Emperor. The day the kitchen gods leave for their weeklong journey is called *Giao Thau.*[11]

Vietnamese families want to make sure the kitchen gods report favorably on their activities to the Jade Emperor. So they place delicious foods and spices on altars in their homes. These offerings are for the kitchen gods before they begin their trip to heaven.[12]

The kitchen gods are said to ride fish on their journey, so many people mark the day by releasing live fish into rivers and lakes. After the kitchen gods leave, families begin preparing for Tet. This period of preparation is called *Tat Nien.*

During Tat Nien, Vietnamese families display altars laden with food in preparation for Tet.

Special Dishes

Vietnamese families spend a lot of time cooking so they will have plenty to eat during Tet. The traditional dish is *banh chung*, which are square-shaped banana leaf cakes filled with rice, beans, and pork. Another popular dish is *banh giay*, which are round, sticky rice cakes.

The streets of Ho Chi Minh City in southern Vietnam are adorned with baskets of fruit during Tet.

Today, many families buy these special treats instead of making them at home because they take a long time to prepare. Some families, though, turn the food preparation into a social occasion. They gather in one kitchen to assemble the cakes, and then boil them for ten or more hours in a large pot of water.[13]

Preparing the House

Fixing up and cleaning the house are important to Tet preparations. Vietnamese families take care of any painting that needs to be done around the house, and clean each room thoroughly. But on the night before the holiday, all cleaning supplies are hidden away. Sweeping and dusting are forbidden on the first and second days of the holiday.

Families in South Vietnam decorate their homes with blooming apricot trees, which represent prosperity in the new year.

On the third day of Tet, floors can be swept, but this chore must be done in a certain way. Also, trash cannot be thrown out until after the second day of Tet. The Vietnamese believe that if trash is swept away or taken out too soon, good luck will disappear for the entire year.

Decorating is also a big part of Tet preparations. Vietnamese families plant a tall bamboo tree in the front of the house. The tree is called *neu.* Bells, gongs, bows, and arrows are hung on the tree to chase away any bad luck of the past. The tree also protects the home from evil spirits that may try to invade while the kitchen gods are away. Neu is a reminder of the legend of how Tet began, when the people tricked the devil and he was banished to the sea.

Fresh Flowers

Many Vietnamese also decorate the inside of the house with fresh flowers. In the South, families decorate with *hoa mai,* or yellow apricot blossoms. In the North, *hoa dao,* or pink peach blossoms, are used. These flowers are often used in much the same way as a Christmas tree.

Many Vietnamese families also decorate with small branches or twigs from trees that have newly sprouted leaves on them. This is part of a Buddhist tradition that symbolizes bringing "fortune-bearing buds" into the home.

Some Vietnamese also bring a kumquat tree into the home. A kumquat is an orange-colored fruit about the size of a plum. In Hanoi and other major cities in Vietnam, merchants line the streets with kumquat trees, each about 2 or 3 feet (0.6 or 0.9 meters) high. The fruit on the tree is said to represent the grandparents and parents of past and present, and the buds represent children and future generations.[14]

Customers crowd the streets to choose the perfect tree. After making their selection, they bring the tree home on a motorbike, a popular mode of transportation. After the year's Tet celebration has concluded, the kumquat trees are planted outside in the family garden or sold to growers who replant them for the next Tet.[15]

Welcoming the Spirits

Getting ready for Tet also means preparing to welcome back the spirits of deceased relatives. Many families have altars in their homes to pay tribute to their ancestors. For Tet, they pay special attention to these altars, placing photos, flowers, candles, and small mementos of the loved ones on the altars. The specially prepared Tet foods are also

In Hanoi, Vietnam, people transport their kumquat trees on motorbikes. The fruit symbolizes past and present generations while the buds symbolize future generations.

placed on the altars. Later, they will be offered to visitors during Tet gatherings.

Vietnamese families try to resolve any issues they may have with family members, business associates, and neighbors. They pay off any debts that may have accumulated during the year. They also buy new clothes to wear.

In the United States, many people stay up late on December 31 and "count down" to midnight, when they welcome the new year with cheers, hugs, and kisses. In Vietnam, the moment when the old year ends and the new year begins is called *Giao Thua. Giao* means "to give," and *Thua* means "to receive."

"By midnight, you set up an altar and make sure everything is clean," said Lan Le, who now lives in San Francisco, California. "You make sure the food is ready for your ancestors and that there are incense and firecrackers."[16]

At midnight, family members gather in front of the altar and perform the family ancestor ritual, called *Gia Tien*. They light joss sticks, which are thin sticks made of dried paste and sweet-smelling wood dust. Then, they invite their ancestors to return for a few days to the world of the living. They also pray, giving thanks to their deceased relatives

During Gia Tien, Vietnamese families light joss, or prayer sticks, to welcome their dead relatives back to earth for a three-day visit.

In Hanoi, Vietnam, women offer incense to their ancestors and pray for a happy and prosperous new year.

who worked hard to enable future generations to have a more prosperous life.

Traditionally, many Vietnamese also set off firecrackers. It is believed that the loud noise scares away the evil spirits. However, firecrackers were banned in Vietnam in the 1990s because there had been numerous injuries during Tet celebrations.

In celebration of Tet, Vietnamese worshippers touch the foot of a Buddha statue as they pray for good fortune.

The Reverend Dominic Nguyen is a priest at Sacred Heart Catholic Church in Dayton, Ohio. "We don't set off firecrackers at Tet," he said of his church. "You have to get permission to do that, and it's too much trouble. [Instead] . . . at *Giao Thua*, we sing, rejoice, and bang gongs and drums."[17]

Tet is here, the Lunar New Year has begun. But the party is not over yet. Indeed, it has just begun.

A four-year-old Vietnamese-American boy celebrates Tet in San Jose, California.

3

Days of Tet

It was Super Bowl Sunday 2006, the day the Pittsburgh Steelers were to play the Seattle Seahawks in the fortieth National Football League championship game. But football was not what brought approximately three hundred people to Thomas Jefferson High School for Science and Technology in Alexandria, Virginia. Instead, the people had gathered in the school cafeteria to celebrate the arrival of Tet. The event was sponsored by several Boy Scout and Girl Scout troops in Virginia, Washington, D.C., and Maryland. These troops are designed especially for children of Vietnamese ancestry. Their regular meetings and special events cover not only the typical scout topics, but also topics of unique interest to Vietnamese families.

Most of the adults at the Tet celebration were naturalized United States citizens. They had immigrated to the United States from Vietnam. A few of the adults were native-born Americans who had adopted children of Vietnamese background. While the scouts were dressed in their uniforms, their younger siblings were decked out in their finest party clothes. Many of the young children wore Vietnamese-styled clothing. The school cafeteria was decorated with a bamboo tree, flowers, and posters the scouts had made, among other items.

Chau Huu Tran and his family were among the attendees that day. Tran grew up in Saigon. After the Vietnam War, he was sent to a refugee camp in Malaysia. He made his way to the United States in 1982 as a teenager, leaving behind his parents and two older sisters. He became a United States citizen and got married. He and his wife have two boys, ages twelve and ten, and a daughter, age seven.

"It is important for my children to know Tet, so they will [know] the traditions," he said. "They . . . think about where their parents came from, and how their parents got here. It is just like them learning history."[1]

The scouts' 2006 Tet festival included reciting the scout oaths in Vietnamese and playing the national anthems of both Vietnam and the United States. It also featured a huge potluck buffet featuring traditional Tet dishes. After lunch, the scouts participated in various activities. They read kitchen god reports they had prepared, and they performed in a violin concert, skits, and dances. One of these dances was the dragon dance.

The dragon dance is an important part of celebrations in all Asian cultures. The mythical creature represents power, dignity, strength, and good luck. The dragon dance is performed in a heavy, bulky costume, and requires many people to work together and perform acrobatic feats in time to a rhythmic drum beat. During the scouts' Tet festival, a Boy Scout and Girl Scout troop each performed a dragon dance.

After an awards ceremony, the scouts' Tet festivities ended around 4:30 P.M. If they had been in Vietnam, however, the party would not be over quite yet. Tet officially lasts for three days, but

The Vietnam War

From its earliest time, Vietnam was under Chinese rule. It gained independence but by the 1800s, had become a colony of France. During World War II, it was occupied by Japan. After World War II, the French tried to reclaim Vietnam, but Vietnam wanted to be independent. Fighting broke out between the French and Vietnamese. Finally, in 1954, France was forced to leave the country, and Vietnam was free to govern itself.

However, Vietnam was divided in two. North Vietnam was communist. To be communist means that the government controls all the land and property, and decides how much money each farmer should have. South Vietnam was not communist. The South Vietnamese wanted to remain free from communist rule, but the North Vietnamese wanted to be one country under communism.

The United States supported South Vietnam's efforts to remain independent of North Vietnam and free of communism. In 1954, the United States government began sending money to South Vietnam to help that government and army. The next year, American service members were sent to South Vietnam to advise and train troops to fight the North Vietnamese troops. In January 1961, the first United States service member was killed in combat in Southeast Asia.[2]

The Vietnam War had officially begun.

The number of American service members in Vietnam increased throughout the next several years. Americans were no longer just training the South Vietnamese; they were fighting alongside them.

At first, many Americans did not understand or even care much about what was happening in Vietnam. But they started paying attention as the number of dead and injured Americans grew higher.

A public opinion poll in September 1967 showed that for the first time since the war began, the majority of Americans did not support United States involvement in Vietnam.[3]

On January 30, 1968, American troops were expecting a temporary cease-fire to honor the Tet holiday. However, the North Vietnamese invaded more than one hundred cities and towns throughout South Vietnam. They also bombed the U.S. Embassy compound in Saigon. Fighting remained fierce for several days. The attacks that sparked the renewed violence came to be known as the Tet Offensive. It was the largest military action in the history of the war.

The Tet Offensive was actually a military failure for North Vietnam. About fifty-five hundred South Vietnamese and American forces were killed, compared with almost seven times as many North Vietnamese troops.[4] Yet the Tet Offensive helped to turn American opinion strongly against the war. Finally, in March 1968, American leaders began peace talks with the North Vietnamese. By October of that year, American service members began returning home. The hope was that the South Vietnamese could defend themselves and remain free of communism.[5]

Finally, in March 1973, five years after the Tet Offensive, the last of the United States combat troops left Vietnam. A month later, almost six hundred United States service members who had been held as prisoners of war were released.

Fighting among the Vietnamese continued, however. Two years after the last American military members returned home, North Vietnamese forces took over South Vietnam. The country became one under communist rule, and it remains that way today.

In Oakland, California, the traditional lion dance starts off the Vietnamese New Year. It is very similar to the dragon dance, but requires less people to perform it.

many families in that country celebrate for an entire week.

Throughout these first days of the Lunar New Year, everyone is on his or her best behavior. The Vietnamese believe their words and actions during the Tet holiday influence how the rest of the year turns out. If harsh words or lies are spoken, bad luck will haunt the new year.

In fact, the Tet moon is a reminder for children to be honest and obedient. A Vietnamese legend tells the story of a beautiful princess who was so curious about life on Earth that she left heaven to check it out. Her father, the king, was so angry that he sent her to the moon as punishment.[6]

"The first three days of Tet have special prayers associated with them," said the Reverend Dominic Nguyen. "The first day we give thanks to God and pray for peace. The second day we pray for our ancestors."[7]

"The third day we pray for our harvests. Following final Mass on Sunday, we'll have a party in the cafeteria for our congregation. After that, we send them off with abundant blessings and best wishes for the new year."[8]

First Day

The first day of Tet is called First Morning, or

Head Day. Family members usually celebrate with the husband's parents. Adult children who live far away from their parents do everything possible to be with their family on this day. The custom of everyone gathering together is called *an Tet*, meaning "eating Tet."

A special ritual on First Morning is called *Mung Tuoi*. It involves children and their grandparents. The children approach their grandparents and fold their arms in front of their chest as a sign of great respect. They tell their grandparents how they have behaved the past year and thank them for their wisdom and guidance. The grandparents, in turn, offer praise and advice for the coming year and then give the children gifts. These gifts are called lucky money, or *li xi*. They are given as birthday gifts and are wrapped in small red envelopes bearing a message, such as "Respectful wishes for the New Year."[9] Throughout the next few days, Vietnamese children will receive more lucky money from other relatives and family friends.

Nhan Thanh Vo, an information technology specialist in the Washington, D.C., area, remembers the lucky money fondly. "I had a lot of lucky money," he said. Vo was born in South Vietnam and grew up in Saigon with five brothers and

In Syracuse, New York, a woman gives a little boy *li xi*, or lucky money, as his birthday gift for the new year.

two sisters. He came to the United States in 1980 as a refugee of the Vietnam War.[10]

After Mung Tuoi, the head of the family steps in front of the altar and presents the offerings to the ancestors. The joss sticks are lit, and the family members pray. They call the names of deceased family members up to five generations, inviting them to return to the world of the living for a few days.[11] When the prayers have concluded, the family dinner is served. Besides banh chung and banh giay, the menu usually includes steamed chicken, bamboo shoot soup, and fresh fruits.[12]

Different parts of Vietnam specialize in other Tet treats, depending on tradition and available products. For example, Vietnamese families in the northern part of the country often serve carp along with cauliflower, or onion fried with pork. The important thing is that all Vietnamese strive to prepare the tastiest and most pleasing dishes to honor and impress not only their ancestors, but also their family members and the many guests they will serve during the next few days. And no matter which dishes are served, hot tea is the typical drink.

After the meal, the family relaxes and waits for the "first-footer." This is the first person in the new year to enter the home. The identity of the first-footer is very important. If the visitor is rich, important, or happy, then it is said the family will have good fortune the rest of the year. Usually, the first-footer is a family member, but sometimes the family will invite a special guest that they believe will bring them even better luck.[13]

Second Day

The second day of Tet is usually spent visiting the maternal grandparents and close friends. Delicious meals are part of every gathering. In the cities, shops that closed on the afternoon before Tet are now open. Some merchants set up lottery stands to entice people who feel lucky for the new year to gamble.

In fact, many people leave their homes not only to shop, but also to gather with friends or neighbors in parks or stroll through the streets. They wear new clothes. Popular colors are red and gold, the colors of the Vietnamese flag. Red also symbolizes good luck and happiness. Many men dress all in black.

"No one locks their doors because everyone's out on the streets mingling," said Gina Hoang, a teenager who left Vietnam when she was five but has heard all about Tet celebrations in her homeland from her relatives.[14]

Third Day

On the third day of Tet, Vietnamese families visit with people in the extended community who are significant to them, such as teachers and co-workers. Again, the visits include sharing a meal.

Children can spend their lucky money on games like *bau cua ca cop*, which is played with dice that feature animals instead of numbers.

Visitors usually say good-bye with a good luck message such as, "I wish that money will flow into your house like water, and out like a turtle."[15] This means they hope that money will be quick to arrive and very slow to leave.

Catherine Diamond is a professor of theater in Taiwan. She traveled to Ho Chi Minh City (formerly known as Saigon) in Vietnam for Tet in 1999. There, she discovered that plays and other live performances are popular with many Vietnamese families during the Tet holiday, even though tickets cost twice as much as the non-holiday price. The themes usually address local concerns or family issues.

"Tet is party time," Diamond said. "Everyone is feasting, visiting friends and relatives, going out to clubs and disco. And yet, when it comes to the stage, the celebration offers scope for serious reflection."[16]

Kenneth Rice is a photographer in Oakland, California. He, too, visited Ho Chi Minh City during a recent Tet celebration. "Photographers are [everywhere], and people pose for photographs everywhere," he said. "The streets are alive with bright colors . . . giant flower arrangements, floats, and people. . . . And there's plenty of food, too:

On the third and final day of Tet, the Vietnamese burn paper to represent the ancestors' return to heaven.

decorated melons and other holiday treats like *banh chung.*"[17]

On the evening of the third day of Tet, the ancestors leave to return to heaven. The Vietnamese symbolize the spirits' departure by burning paper. They believe their ancestors will take the ashes with them on their journey back to heaven. The Tet holiday is now officially over, but many Vietnamese families take the rest of the week off before returning to their usual routine.

Many people welcome the new year at midnight on December 31. But whether it is because of an ancestral link or simply an interest in the culture, more and more people are also celebrating the Lunar New Year. They are borrowing elements of traditional Asian celebrations and mixing them with American ways.

"Glutinous Rice Cake Peddler," illustration from *Calls, Sounds and Merchandise of the Peking Street Peddlers*, by Samuel V. Constant, 1937 (colour litho).

4

Symbols of Tet

Legends are stories passed down from generation to generation, and there are many legends that are associated with Tet traditions. The following legend explains the significance of the square- and round-shaped cakes that are eaten on this special holiday.

Once there was a ruler named King Hung Vuong II. He was very popular because he was kind and fair. He made earth and sky cakes every year to offer to the ancestors at Tet. The earth cakes were shaped into squares, and the sky cakes were shaped into spheres. The king's cakes were the best in all the kingdom, and so people wondered if he had a special way of making them. One year, the king invited all the people to watch him make the cakes. As he made them, he told them the story of Lieu.

Lieu was one of many sons of King Hung Vuong I. He lived with his mother, who preferred the simple life, so he did not have nearly as much money and goods as the other princes in the kingdom.

One day, the king ruled that each prince should make a special dish to offer to the ancestors on Tet. He said the special dish should express thanks. Lieu did not know how to cook. His mother had recently died, so she could not help him. And Lieu did not have money to buy fancy ingredients. Lieu was very discouraged, so he decided not to enter the contest.

That night, after he fell asleep, his mother appeared to him in a dream. "My son, you have misunderstood the king," she said. "He does not demand wealth or fancy skill as a cook. He is looking only for a good heart, and that I know you possess."[1] In the dream, she pointed to the rice fields with one hand, and to the sky with the other.

When Lieu woke up, he thought about the dream. He believed his mother was showing him the rice fields as an image of Earth, and the sky as an image of heaven. Earth nourished the people, and heaven watched over them.[2]

Lieu decided to make square-shaped cakes to represent Mother Earth. He boiled sweet rice, mashed it into a paste, and then shaped the paste into squares. He filled the cakes with beans and onions to represent gifts from the earth. Then he wrapped the cakes in fresh banana leaves and tied them with thin bamboo strips.

Lieu made another pot of sweet rice, mashed it into a paste, and shaped it into spheres. These spheres represented the sky. He placed the cakes on fresh green leaves. Lieu's dishes were made simply and without any waste.

The next day, Lieu took his cakes to the palace. His offerings looked simple and plain next to the others. The king examined and tasted each dish, and asked questions about its preparation. Finally, the king came to Lieu. He tasted the cakes but did not ask Lieu any questions. Later, Lieu was summoned to the palace. The king said that by looking at and tasting Lieu's cakes, he knew Lieu had the heart, humility, and talent to protect the kingdom and honor the ancestors.[3] Lieu would be the next king because he "is wise," the king said. "He relied on Vietnamese ingredients, and he cooked cakes that symbolize the harmony of heaven and earth."[4]

So Lieu became King Hung Vuong II. He taught the people how to make the cakes, emphasizing that great cooking skills and fancy ingredients were not important. Instead, the most important thing is a heart filled with love and gratitude. To this day, Vietnamese families offer these cakes on their ancestral altars at Tet to show that they are filled with love for their relatives and their homeland.[5]

Legend of Sticky Rice

Another legend surrounds the glutinous, or sticky, rice (*gao nep*) used to make Tet specialties. This legend is a lesson on support and love among siblings. Once there were two orphaned brothers who were very close to each other. The older brother got married and had children, while the younger brother remained single. They harvested rice from the same field, and always divided the rice equally between the two households.

Eventually, however, the rice reserves became very low. The younger brother became worried that his older brother's family would not have enough

Today, vendors sell bundles of sticky rice wrapped in leaves for the New Year celebration.

to eat. So he decided to take several bushels of his own rice and sneak it into his brother's storage bin. The older brother, meanwhile, became worried that the younger brother was all alone and would have no one to help him if he ran out of rice. So the older brother decided to take a portion of his own rice and sneak it into the younger brother's storage bin.

The two brothers met in the storeroom. When they each realized what the other was doing, they cried tears of happiness and love. The falling tears made the grains of rice more delicious than any other type.[6]

Sweeping as Bad Luck

Cleaning is a very big part of preparing for Tet, but during the holiday, sweeping and taking out the trash cannot be done until after the second day. The Vietnamese believe that if these activities happen too soon, good luck will disappear for the entire year. This belief is based on the legend of the traveling merchant and his wife.

Once there was a traveling merchant who fell in love with a beautiful young woman. She fell in love with him, too, and they were married. The woman brought the man good luck; he became wealthier and wealthier. Meanwhile, she devoted herself to keeping their house spotless.

One day, the man brought home a very expensive antique vase. He treasured it, but his wife accidentally broke it while cleaning. The man became so angry with his wife that she became fearful of him. She hid in a pile of trash that she had compiled in her cleaning.

The man did not know his wife was in the trash. He ordered the pile of trash removed from their home because it reminded him of his wife's carelessness. His wife was never seen again, and with her absence, the man's good luck disappeared. He became very poor.[7]

The Kitchen Gods

Vietnamese people believe that three kitchen gods, or Tao Quan, are present in the kitchen of every home. These gods represent the spirits of two men and a woman. The legend surrounding them has to do with love and noble motives.

Once there lived a woodcutter and his wife. The woodcutter was a good man, but he grew very discouraged because they were so poor. Eventually, he became angry and violent. His wife became fearful of his outbursts and one night, she ran out of their house and into the woods. She wandered for weeks until, finally, she came to a hunter's cabin. The hunter was very kind and took her in, and eventually, they were married.

One day, the hunter was out in the forest searching for birds to shoot and eat for the Tet celebration. His wife was home alone. A beggar knocked on the door and asked for food, and the woman invited him in and prepared him a meal.

As he ate, she recognized that the beggar was her former husband, the woodcutter.

Suddenly, she heard the footsteps of the hunter returning home. The woman panicked and hid the woodcutter under a big pile of hay. The hunter entered the cottage and before the woman could stop him, set the pile of hay on fire so that he could cook the birds. He did not know the woodcutter was hiding there.

The woman, feeling guilty, panicked, and grief stricken, jumped into the fire so that she could die with the woodcutter. The hunter tried to pull her out, but it was too late. Thinking that he must have done something terrible to cause her to act so desperately, he, too, jumped into the fire. Their three spirits became the Kitchen Gods.

Watermelons

Vietnamese often eat watermelon during Tet festivities. They believe that the redder the melon is, the more good luck they will have. They recall the legend of An Tiem, an orphan who became a helper on a merchant ship. One day, An Tiem went with the ship's captain to pay respect to the king. The king was impressed with the boy and decided to raise him as his own son.

In Ho Chi Minh City, Vietnam, vendors bring many baskets of watermelons to sell at a fruit market. The Vietnamese eat watermelons during Tet and believe that a redder fruit on the inside means good luck for the new year.

When An Tiem grew up, he married the king's daughter, Oanh. An Tiem spoke several languages, so the king put him in charge of trade with foreign countries. An Tiem was very successful, and some in the kingdom became jealous. They told the king that An Tiem had said that he had not needed the king's help to become successful.

The king called for An Tiem and asked him about it. "Father, I am not ungrateful," An Tiem said. "I know . . . that I could not be where I am today without all your generous support. I did say, however, that I enjoy good fruits in this life because of good deeds I did in former lives."[8]

Angry, the king asked An Tiem if he thought he could survive if he were banished to a deserted island. An Tiem said that yes, he thought he could. So An Tiem, his wife, and child were sent to live on an island with nothing but a few provisions.

On the island, An Tiem discovered a patch of unusual melons. They were very red with black seeds, and very sweet. An Tiem took several of the seeds and planted them, and more melons grew. Then one day, a foreign ship arrived on the island and traded some of its goods for some of the delicious melons. An Tiem planted more melons, and many more grew. His crop was bountiful, and the ship returned to trade with him. Soon, he had a very successful business and was able to build a grand house.

After four years, An Tiem sent some melons to the king to let him know how he had fared. The king realized he had been wrong and called for him to return. "Your words were not those of an ungrateful son . . . but the words of one who believes in taking responsibility for his own actions," he said.[9]

An Tiem and his family returned to the kingdom and brought with them many seeds to grow melons throughout the kingdom.

* * *

These are just a few of the Vietnamese legends, which usually focus on nature, family, love, and understanding. Knowing these legends and passing them on to the next generation help to enrich the lives of the Vietnamese and to make the Tet holiday even more meaningful.

This shop in Vietnam displays ornaments for Tet.

Old and the New

The Vietnamese population in the United States is significant. Today, approximately 995,000 Vietnamese immigrants and their American-born children live in the United States.[1] The total Asian population in the United States is approximately 11.8 million. This figure includes not only those with Vietnamese ancestry, but also people who emigrated from China, Japan, Korea, and other Asian nations.[2] Experts predict that by the year 2030, one out of every four immigrants to the

In Westminster, California, a six-year-old boy participates in a Tet festival by wearing a colorful mask. California is home to a large number of Vietnamese immigrants and their families who continue to practice their ethnic customs and celebrations.

United States will be from an Asian or Hispanic country.[3] These immigrants bring with them the traditions of their home countries to share with their new neighbors.

The largest Asian populations are found in the California cities of Los Angeles and San Francisco, and in New York City. Indeed, about 40 percent of all Asian immigrants have settled in these three cities. Asian populations are also growing significantly in Las Vegas, Nevada; Atlanta, Georgia; Phoenix, Arizona; and Dallas and Houston, in Texas.[4]

When looking only at Vietnamese immigrants, the largest population is found in Southern California. Significant numbers are also located in Houston and Dallas; the suburbs of Washington, D.C.; and the states of Washington, Pennsylvania, Minnesota, Massachusetts, New York, and Illinois.[5]

Those with Asian heritage settled in the United States by fate, fortune, or opportunity. And while undoubtedly they have embraced the American lifestyle, they do not want to forget their past. They have brought the elements of their ancestral culture to their new home, incorporating the traditions of yesterday with the lifestyle of today.

Our Fellow Americans

Today, approximately 995,000 Vietnamese immigrants and their American-born children live in the United States.[6] Most of the Vietnamese came from South Vietnam, which was overtaken by North Vietnam in 1975.

The Southeast Asia Resource Action Center has classified those who arrived in the United States as follows:

*Approximately 135,000 Vietnamese fled to the United States when Saigon fell to the Communists in April 1975. Most in this group were former South Vietnamese military and government officials and their families. It also included Vietnamese who had worked for United States officials during the war and their family members.

*Conditions grew very bad in Vietnam in the late 1970s, causing thousands to escape by boat. Exact figures of these so-called "boat people" are unknown, and it is believed that many died at sea. The survivors reached refugee camps in Thailand, Malaysia, Indonesia, the Philippines, and Hong Kong before being admitted to the United States and other countries.

*Under pressure from the United Nations, the Vietnamese government allowed some of its citizens to leave. Those who were allowed "orderly departure" had to have relatives who had resettled elsewhere.

*Approximately 100,000 Amerasians, or children born to Vietnamese mothers and American service member fathers during the war years, were allowed to immigrate.[7]

In Garden City, Kansas, middle school students perform a traditional Vietnamese fan dance to bring in 2002, the Year of the Horse according to the Buddhist Zodiac.

For the Vietnamese, the most important tradition is Tet. Living in the United States means the Vietnamese must follow the Gregorian calendar for their work and school schedules. On the Gregorian calendar, the new year officially begins on January 1. But many Vietnamese also mark Tet, which occurs sometime between January 19 and February 20 each year. Many Asian communities hold special celebrations to welcome the Lunar New Year. They invite Americans from all backgrounds to participate.

Texas

Thanh Tran lives in Arlington, Texas. The city is part of Tarrant County, where the Vietnamese population totals approximately 24,000. When Tran was younger, he lived in Vietnam. He remembers celebrating Tet by dancing through the city streets of Hue holding a paper lion's head on a stick.[8]

Tran is now a member of the Vietnamese Youth Association's Lion Dancing Troupe. He takes part in Arlington's annual Tet festival by performing in the lion dance. The lion dance is similar to the dragon dance.

"We dance to scare away evil spirits and to bring luck to people and businesses," he said.

In Austin, Texas, young boys bring in 2006, the Year of the Dog, with the rhythmic beat of taiko drumming during a Tet festival.

"It's really kind of an aerobic and martial art combined."[9]

Andy Nguyen is chairman of the Vietnamese American Community of Tarrant County. "From a cultural standpoint, this is an opportunity for the young people of the Vietnamese community to witness ancestral ceremonies, see people from different backgrounds and find something in common," he said.[10]

Taho Phan also performs in the lion dance. She does so "to keep the tradition alive and to bring the luck and joy to people."[11]

Traditionally, the city of Houston, Texas, celebrates Tet in a big way. "Ten years ago, the Chinese people [in the community] celebrated but on a very small scale," said Yali Zou, director of the Asian-American Studies Center at the University of Houston. "Now Chinese people, the Asian-American community and the whole society recognize this kind of celebration."[12]

Zou said she believes it is the beauty of the tradition that makes everyone want to celebrate. "The music, the dance, the sounds, the culture . . . People see this beauty, they enjoy this beauty, and then they want to protect this beauty."[13]

"For the longest time, [the Lunar New Year] was a very cultural celebration" unique to the Asian community, said Bonnie Gutierrez, who is co-owner of a Houston-based fortune cookie company. "It's kind of amazing . . . that people would find the time to find out when [the Lunar New Year] is and have a celebration."[14]

New York City

Lan Tran Cao is another Vietnamese-American citizen who has incorporated the Tet traditions into her new lifestyle. Cao is the owner of Vietcafe, a restaurant in the Tribeca area of New York City. Every year, she holds an annual Tet party in a gallery attached to her restaurant. In 2005, more than forty families attended. Many of them were Americans who had adopted children who had been born in Vietnam.[15]

Cao's party featured banh chung, of course, as well as a play describing the significance of the dish. As Cao and her sister prepared the banh chung, they recalled that when they were growing up in Vietnam, their family made about seventy cakes to eat during the Tet holidays.[16]

Hugh Duthie is the owner of a Vietnamese housewares shop in New York City. For Tet 2003, he invited several friends over. Friends who are chefs helped him prepare traditional Tet dishes. Duthie explained the meaning of the holiday to his friends and gave them lucky money.[17]

Florida

The Asian community in Orlando, Florida, held a parade to mark Tet 2006, the Year of the Dog. Events included the lion dance through the Asian business district and a special Mass at St. Philip Phan Van Minh. This church was the first Roman Catholic church in Orlando.

"The New Year to the Asian community is a big thing," said Karen Mai Khanh, who attended Mass in traditional Asian dress.[18]

California

At the University of California at Los Angeles, the Vietnamese Language and Cultural Group's 2006 Tet festival featured two fashion shows. One showcased traditional Vietnamese clothing, and the other mixed traditional Asian fashions with those from other cultures. The festival also included skits, singing, and traditional food and games. Kim Tai, who helped organize the show, said participating in the Tet celebration "allows us to remain in touch with our culture and not forget our roots."[19]

The city of Saratoga, California, held its first Lunar New Year celebration in 2006. The city was turning fifty years old that year and wanted to sponsor a variety of activities to mark the occasion. City officials chose the Lunar New Year because the city's Asian population had grown tremendously. It was approximately 5 percent of the total population in 1980; today, it is approximately 29 percent. "It just helps us to relate to each other better after we learn about each other's cultures," said Councilwoman Kathleen King.[20]

West Virginia

In Charleston, West Virginia, Trinity Nicholas held a Lunar New Year celebration for other families who, like hers, had adopted children from Korea. "We may never know who our children's biological ancestors are, but we know that without them we would not have these babies," she said. "We owe it to their birth mothers . . . the ones who loved them first. And we owe it to their ancestors. We cannot let them down. . . . So today we honor them."[21]

Official Recognition

As Lunar New Year celebrations have grown in popularity in the United States, the holiday is getting some official recognition. In recent years, the United States Postal Service issued a series of commemorative stamps designed after the twelve animals in the Buddhist zodiac. United States presidents have traditionally sent official greetings to the Asian community to mark the Lunar New Year.

"In marking this special occasion, you help preserve your rich heritage and ensure your values of family, faith, and respect for tradition are passed on to future generations," said President George W. Bush in Lunar New Year greetings on February 8, 2005, which ushered in the Year of the Rooster.[22]

During a Tet parade in California, these teens carry a South Vietnamese flag with three stripes representing north, central, and south Vietnam.

"This observance also reminds all Americans of the unique fabric that makes up our country," the president said, "and the diversity that has made our nation stronger and better."[23]

In 1994, the city of San Francisco, California, agreed to close its schools on the Lunar New Year. Today, Asian groups across the nation are seeking to make the Lunar New Year a federal holiday in which public schools would close and employees would get the day off with pay.

"This is about respect for our culture," said Henry Lau, cofounder of the Maryland Coalition for Recognition of the Asian Lunar New Year. "The New Year is the most important festival in our culture, and that needs to be acknowledged."[24]

The growing interest in the Lunar New Year has sparked interest in visiting Vietnam. For many years, the country was closed to tourism. But in the past several years, millions of people have become intrigued by the country and its traditions, including Tet. They have made Vietnam one of the top vacation destinations.

Making New Memories

I t seemed an unlikely vacation destination for Senator John McCain of Arizona, his wife, Cindy, and their thirteen-year-old son, Jack. They were visiting Hanoi, the capital of Vietnam. McCain had visited seven times previously, but it was the first time he had brought his teenaged son along. McCain wanted to show Jack where he spent several grim years of his life, not knowing if he would ever return to the United States.

Today, shoppers browse fruits and vegetables along a street in Hanoi.

McCain was a navy pilot during the Vietnam War. His plane had been shot down during a bombing run over Hanoi. McCain was captured and sent to Hanoi as a prisoner of war (POW). He spent almost seven years confined in the infamous "Hanoi Hilton," the sprawling compound where he and approximately three hundred other POWs had been held.[1]

After the war, the Vietnamese tore down most of the compound to build a luxury hotel and office complex. However, they preserved part of the compound as a museum. It was here where McCain took his son in April 2000. Even though McCain had been a POW, he was a strong supporter of the people of Vietnam. He wanted the United States to establish better relations with the Southeast Asian country. McCain said one of the reasons he made that eighth trip to Vietnam was to "commemorate the beginning and continuation of a new relationship with the United States and Vietnam."[2]

The Vietnam War ended in 1973, but for many years after that Vietnam was closed to the rest of the world. The country became one under communism in 1975, when South Vietnam was overtaken by North Vietnam. Thousands of Vietnamese fled to a better life in the United States and other countries. For those who remained, life was very harsh politically as well as economically.

By the late 1980s, conditions slowly began improving. The Vietnamese government recognized that for the country to survive, it needed to become part of the global community. It changed some of its policies to make that happen. The country remains communist, but the government has listened to some of the calls for changes to make life better for the Vietnamese people.

In July 1995, President William Clinton announced that the United States would re-establish diplomatic relations with Vietnam. Five years later, in October 2000, Clinton traveled to Vietnam. He became the first United States president to visit that country since the Vietnam War ended in 1973.[3]

Since Clinton's historic visit, millions of other people have also visited Vietnam. Many of these visitors, like McCain, were Vietnam veterans who wanted to return to the land that had had such a significant impact on their life. But nonveterans also took trips to Vietnam. In fact, approximately 3.5 million people from other countries visited Vietnam in 2005, an 18.4 percent increase from the previous year.[4]

Intrigued by its exotic beauty and historical significance, millions of people from all over the world visit Vietnam. Its tourism industry continues to grow.

Tourism to Vietnam is expected to increase in the years ahead. According to a recent report, Vietnam's travel and tourism sector is expected to grow approximately 8 percent in the next several years. If that prediction holds true, it will have the sixth-highest tourism growth rate in the world.[5]

Visitors to Vietnam report that the landscape is lush and beautiful, the food is delicious, and the people are very friendly and gentle.[6] "During a recent visit to Vietnam with a group of educators . . . I was astounded to see another Vietnam with a

People on bicycles ride down the Ho Chi Minh Trail, a popular tourist destination that was used to transport supplies during the Vietnam War.

future, not backward orientation," said Ellen Kronowitz, a college professor in California. "The people there look to the future and not to the past."[7]

"Everyone seems to be coming to Vietnam, the new land of opportunity," said a man named Tsu, who works as a hotel receptionist in the town of Hoi An.[8]

One popular destination is the Ho Chi Minh Trail, which played an important role in the Vietnam War. The North Vietnamese used the heavily jungled trail to transport soldiers and supplies to battlefields in South Vietnam.[9] Now, visitors can ride bikes, drive cars, or even walk on many parts of the trail. It begins in Hanoi, the capital, and winds

The Vietnamese flag

through battlefields and cemeteries, tribal villages, the ancient royal city of Hue, picturesque seaports, and rice-farming villages. The trail ends in Ho Chi Minh City, which was known as Saigon when it was the capital of South Vietnam.[10]

Vietnam remains a poor country, with many challenges ahead. But for those looking for

Picturesque scenes like these fishing boats in the port of Phu Quoc attract adventurous travelers eager for new cultural experiences.

adventure and a chance to experience another culture, a trip to this Southeast Asian country is a wonderful possibility.

For those who cannot travel away from home, there are opportunities to experience the Vietnamese culture here in the United States by attending a Tet festival. Vietnamese communities in many large metropolitan areas hold these festivals so that all people can experience the cultural, spiritual, and national significance of this holiday. Aside from sampling new foods, hearing new stories, and taking in new sights, you just may get good luck for the entire new year.

The "First-Footer"

On Tet, Vietnamese families eagerly await the arrival of the "first-footer," the first person in the Lunar New Year to enter the family's home. The Vietnamese believe that if the visitor is rich, important, or happy, then the family will have good fortune for the rest of the year.

Think about the people you know and the people you admire. Who would you pick as the first-footer to your house on Tet? Write a short paragraph naming the person you would choose as first-footer, and explain why you chose that person.

GLOSSARY

bilingual—Able to speak two languages.

carp—A large, freshwater fish with soft fins.

cease-fire—A military order to stop fighting.

communism—A system where government controls property and organizes the economic and social system under common ownership.

emigrant—A person who leaves his or her country to live elsewhere.

glutinous—Sticky; having qualities of glue.

immigrant—A person who comes to a country to live permanently.

legend—A story that is handed down from generation to generation.

lunar—Relating to the moon.

myth—A story told to explain a view or purpose.

obedient—Willingness to yield or cooperate.

refugee—A person who flees to another country to escape danger or persecution.

solar—Relating to the sun.

subtropical—A region with high temperatures and frost-free conditions.

superstition—A belief or practice resulting from ignorance, fear of the unknown, or a false belief.

temperate—Mild, moderate.

ubiquitous—Being everywhere at the same time.

waning—Decreasing.

waxing—Increasing.

CHAPTER NOTES

◆ **Chapter 1.** **Ancient Tradition**

1. "Tet Legends: The Neu Tree," Lunar New Year Vietnam Style, n.d.,<www.vnstyle.vdc.com/vn/lunar_newyear/tet_leeng/cayneu.htm> (July 18, 2005).

2. "Who Was Buddha?" The Friends of the Western Buddhist Order, n.d., <www.fwbo.org/buddha.html> (September 18, 2006).

3. Khalid Moss, "For Vietnamese, Tonight's a Warmup to Tet: After the Countdown, Plans Begin for the Lunar New Year," *Dayton Daily News*, December 31, 2005, p. E–3.

4. Ellen L. Kronowitz, "Creating New Images of Vietnam: Celebrating Tet in the Middle-school Classroom," *The Social Studies Teacher*, January 11, 1995, vol. 86, p. 30.

5. Mason Florence, *Vietnam* (Footscray, Victoria, Australia: Lonely Planet Publications, 2003), p. 35.

6. "Country Guide: Vietnam," *BBC Weather Centre website*, n.d., <http://www.bbc.co.uk/weather/world/country_guides/results.shtml?tt=TT002920> (October 18, 2006).

7. Nick Ray and Wendy Yanagihara, Vietnam (Footscray, Victoria, Australia: Lonely Planet Publications, 2005), p. 47.

8. "The Lunar Calendar in Vietnam," Wayto vietnam.com, 2005, <http://www.waytovietnam. com/culture-detail.asp?qCLId=101> (October 18, 2006).

9. Ray and Yanagihara, p. 47.

10. "The Year of the Rooster: What Kind of Rooster Are You?" *Lunar New Year Vietnam Style*, n.d., <www.vnstyle.vdc.com/vn/lunar_newyear/ind ex.html> (July 18, 2005).

11. James Pringle, "Year of the Monkey Marks a Turning Point in Vietnam; MEANWHILE," *International Herald Tribune*, January 22, 2004, p. 7.

12. "U.S. Postage Stamp Celebrates Lunar New Year: 'Year of the Horse' is Tenth Stamp in Series Commemorating Chinese New Year," *US Newswire*, February 1, 2002, <web2.infotrac. galenet.com/itw/infomark/> (April 7, 2006).

13. Letha Hadady, "Chinese Astrology," *China Sprout*, 1999–2006, <http://www.chinasprout. com/htm/community.html?section=community &topic=staticpages&id=59> (October 23, 2006).

14. Author's interview with Antoinette Nguyen, February 10, 2006.

15. Tracy Ward, "Tet, the Vietnamese New Year, A Lesson Plan for Grades 4–6," *Adopt Vietnam*,

n.d., <www.adoptvietnam.org/vietnamese/ tet-lessonplan.htm> (March 30, 2006).

♦ **Chapter 2. Honoring the Living and the Dead**

1. Author's interview with Antoinette Nguyen, February 10, 2006.
2. Ibid.
3. Ibid.
4. Ibid.
5. Ibid.
6. Ibid.
7. Audrey Seah, *Cultures of the World: Vietnam* (New York: Marshall Cavendish, 1994), pp. 81–83.
8. Ibid.
9. Ibid.
10. Author's interview with Chau Huu Tran, February 10, 2006.
11. "Tet Legends: The Origin of Tao Quan, the Three Kitchen Gods," n.d.,<vnstyle.vdc.com. vn/lunar_newyear/tet_legend/index.html> (July 18, 2005).
12. "Tet: No Kris Kringle, Evergreens, Presents, or Fruitcake, Just the Jade Emperor, Hoa Doa, Li Xi, and Mut," *Indiana University's Asian American Association,* January 31, 2006, <http://www.indiana.edu/~aaa/?p=53> (October 18, 2006).

13. Peggy Grodinsky, "Vietnamese New Year: Everybody Have Fun Tonight, Everybody Banh Chung Tonight: Making Holiday Rice Cakes is a Family Affair," *Houston Chronicle*, January 25, 2006, p. 4.

14. Host Bob Edwards, Michael Sullivan reporting, "Vietnam Celebrates Tet New Year," Morning Edition, National Public Radio, *NPR.org*, broadcast January 22, 2004, <http://www.npr.org/templates/story/story.php?storyId=1611043> (January 3, 2006).

15. Ibid.

16. Cicero A. Estrella, "Lunar New Year a Multicultural Celebration," *San Francisco Chronicle*, January 22, 2004, p. A–1.

17. Khalid Moss, "For Vietnamese, Tonight's a Warmup to Tet: After the Countdown, Plans Begin for the Lunar New Year," *Dayton Daily News*, December 31, 2005, p. E–3.

◆ **Chapter 3. Days of Tet**

1. Author's interview with Chau Huu Tran, February 10, 2006.

2. Laura S. Jeffrey, *Fifty Years of Military Life: Army Times Anniversary Edition* (Springfield, Va.: Times Journal Co., 1990), pp. 18–19.

3. Ibid.

4. Ibid.

5. Ibid.

6. "Holidays of the Vietnamese," www.ask.asia.org, n.d., <www.askasia.org/Vietnam_Challenge/curric/middle/20.htm> (July 18, 2005

7. Khalid Moss, "For Vietnamese, Tonight's a Warmup to Tet: After the Countdown, Plans Begin for the Lunar New Year," *Dayton Daily News*, December 31, 2005, p. E–3.

8. Ibid.

9. "Sequence of Tet: First Morning," *Lunar New Year Vietnam Style*, n.d., <www.vnstyle.vdc.com/vn/lunar_newyear/sequence_tet/first morning.html> (July 18, 2005).

10. Author's interview with Nhan Thanh Vo, February 11, 2006.

11. "Sequence of Tet: First Morning."

12. Ibid.

13. Tracy Ward, "Tet, the Vietnamese New Year, A Lesson Plan for Grades 4–6," *Adopt Vietnam*, n.d., <www.adoptvietnam.org/vietnamese/tet-lessonplan.htm> (March 30, 2006).

14. Cicero A. Estrella, "Lunar New Year a Multi-cultural Celebration," *San Francisco Chronicle*, January 22, 2004, p. A–1.

15. Ward.

16. Catherine Diamond, "During Tet, Postwar Reflection," *American Theatre*, September 1, 1999, p. 61.

17. Kenneth Rice, "Seeking Good Fortune: Vietnam's Tet Celebration," *The World & I,* March 1, 1995, vol. 10, *Articles in Magazines,* 2005, <http://www.articlesinmagazines.com/ CULTURE/Seeking_Good_Fortune_Vietnams_ Tet_Cele.htm> (January 4, 2006).

◆ **Chapter 4. Symbols of Tet**

1. Thich Nhat Hanh, *A Taste of Earth and other Legends of Vietnam* (Berkeley, Calif.: Parallax Press, 1993), p. 53.
2. Ibid.
3. Ibid., p. 56.
4. Peggy Grodinsky, "Vietnamese New Year: Everybody Have Fun Tonight, Everybody Banh Chung Tonight," *Houston Chronicle,* January 25, 2006, p. 4.
5. Nhat Hanh, p. 56.
6. "Tet Legends: Heart Makes Glutinous Rice," *VN Media, Vietnamese Data Communications Company,* n.d., <http://www.vnstyle.vdc.com. vn/lunar_newyear/tet_legend/gaonep.htm> (July 18, 2005).
7. "Tet Legends: Prohibition Against Throwing Out Trash at Tet," VnMedia, *Vietnam Data Communications Company,* 2000, <http://www.vn style.vdc.com.vn/lunar_newyear/tet_legend/ camhotracngaytet.htm> (July 18, 2005).
8. Nhat Hanh, p. 57.

9. Ibid., p. 62.

Chapter 5. Old and the New

1. "Vietnamese Refugees," *Southeast Asia Resource Action Center*, n.d., <http://www.searac.org/vietref.html> (October 18, 2006).

2. "Table 1. Population by Sex and Age, for Asian Alone and White Alone, Not Hispanic: March 2004," *United States Census Bureau*, March 2006, <http://www.census.gov/population/socdemo/race/api/ppl-184/tab1.html> (April 8, 2006).

3. William F. Frey, "The United States Population: Where the New Immigrants Are," *U.S. Society and Values*, vol. 4, no. 2, June 1999, pp. 25–28, <http://usinfo.state.gov/journals/itsv/0699/ijse/ijse0699.pdf> (October 18, 2006).

4. Ibid.

5. "Vietnamese Refugees."

6. Ibid.

7. Ibid.

8. Neil Strassman, "Tet Festival to Mark Lunar New Year," *Fort Worth-Star Telegram*, January 29, 2006, distributed by KnightRidder/Tribune Business News, p. BB1.

9. Ibid.

10. Ibid.

11. Ibid.

11. Ibid.

12. Kristin Finan, "Year of the Dog: As the Asian Lunar Celebration Begins, More People in Houston Are Taking Part and in Some Not-So-Traditional Ways," *Houston Chronicle*, January 29, 2006, p. B–1.
13. Ibid.
14. Ibid.
15. Dana Bowen, "Traditional Flavors of the Lunar New York," *The New York Times*, January 25, 2006, p. F–3.
16. Ibid.
17. Linda Lee, "Happy New Year! (Practice Makes Perfect)," *The New York Times*, February 9, 2003, section 8, p. 9.
18. Sandra Pedicini, "Asians Welcome New Year: The Year of the Dog Arrives With a Special Mass and Festivities," *Orlando Sentinel*, January 30, 2006, distributed by Knight-Ridder/Tribune Business News, p. B3.
19. Jackie Brosamer, "UCLA Culture Night Rings in Vietnamese New Year," *Daily Bruin online*, February 6, 2006, <http://www.dailybruin.ucla.edu/news/articles.asp?ID=35773> (October 18, 2006).
20. Truong Phuoc Khanh, "City Observes 50th Birthday With Multicultural Events—Agricultural Past, Lunar New Year Joined," *San Jose Mercury News*, February 6, 2006, distributed by Knight-Ridder/Tribune Business News, p. 3B.

21. Trinity Nicholas, "Lunar New Year: Adoptive Families Help Their Children Celebrate Traditional Korean Holiday," *Charleston Daily Mail*, February 1, 2006, p. D–1.

22. "Message on the Observance of the Lunar New Year, 2005," 2005 U.S. Government Printing Office, Source: Weekly Compilation of Presidential Documents, February 14, 2005, vol. 41, i6, p. 197, <http://www.gpoaccess.gov/wcomp/v41no06.html> (April 7, 2006).

23. Ibid.

24. Amit R. Paley, "A Date With Tradition: Chinese New Year Ushers in Quest for Official Holiday Recognition," *The Washington Post*, January 29, 2006, p. C–1.

◆ **Chapter 6.** **Making New Memories**

1. "McCain Returns to Vietnam for a Tour, Including Stop at Former Prison," The Associated Press, April 24, 2000, *Neil Mishalov's Web site*, 2006, <http://www.mishalov.com/Vietnam_McCain.html> (October 19, 2006).

2. Ibid.

3. "Statement of Virginia B. Foote, President, U.S.–Vietnam Trade Council; Testimony Before the Subcommittee on Trade of the House Committee on Ways and Means; Hearing on Renewal of President's Waiver for Vietnam From the Jackson-Vanik Freedom of Emigration

Requirements," *Committee on Ways and Means*, July 18, 2002, <http://waysandmeans.house. gov/legacy/trade/107cong/7-18-02/7-18 foote.htm> (October 19, 2006).

4. "Vietnam's Tourism Booming," *CDNN–Cyber Diver News Network,* March 20, 2006, <http:// www.cdnn.info/news/travel/t060320a.html> (April 7, 2006).

5. Ibid.

6. Arthur Asa Berger, *Vietnam Tourism* (Bing-hamton, N.Y.: Haworth Press, Inc., 2005), pp. 15–17.

7. Ellen L. Kronowitz, "Creating New Images of Vietnam: Celebrating Tet in the Middle-school Classroom," *The Social Studies Teacher*, January 11, 1995, vol. 86, p. 29.

8. Brigitte Bertrou Seligman, "Vietnam's Living Museum," *The World & I*, June 1, 1996, vol. 11, p. 138.

9. Denis D. Gray, "Trail of Tears and Tourism in Vietnam: Ho Chi Minh Trail Evolves From Soldiers' Road to Visitors' Highway," Associated Press, posted on Post-Gazette.com travel, August 7, 2005, <www.post-gazette.com/pg/ 05219/548897.stm> (April 7, 2006).

10. Ibid.

FURTHER READING

Books

Anderson, Dale. *The Tet Offensive: Turning Point of the Vietnam War.* Minneapolis, Minn.: Compass Point Books, 2005.

Englar, Mary. *Vietnam: A Question and Answer Book.* Mankato, Minn.: Capstone Press, 2007.

Garland, Sherry. *Children of the Dragon: Selected Tales From Vietnam.* San Diego, Calif.: Harcourt, 2001.

Kalman, Bobbie. *Vietnam. The Culture.* New York: Crabtree Publishing Company, 2002.

Parker, Lewis K. *Why Vietnamese Immigrants Came to America.* New York: PowerKids Press, 2003.

Simpson, Judith. *Vietnam.* Broomall, Pa.: Mason Crest Publishers, 2003.

INTERNET ADDRESSES

About Tet
<http://www.familyculture.com/holidays/
tet.htm>

Learn more about Tet at this site.

Vietnam
<http://www.geographia.com/vietnam/>

Read about the history and culture of Vietnam.

INDEX